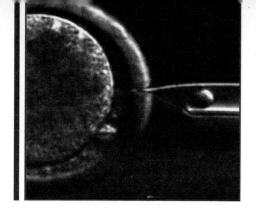

The Debate Over Human Cloning

A Pro/Con Issue

David Goodnough

HOT
PRO/CON
ISSUES

Enslow Publishers, Inc.

40 Industrial Road   PO Box 38
Box 398   Aldershot
Berkeley Heights, NJ 07922   Hants GU12 6BP
USA   UK

http://www.enslow.com

Library of Congress Cataloging-in-Publication Data

Goodnough, David.
    The debate over human cloning : a pro/con issue / David Goodnough.
        p. cm. — (Hot pro/con issues)
    Summary: Provides an overview of the technology and history of
cloning and presents arguments for and against human cloning.
    Includes bibliographical references and index.
    ISBN 0-7660-1818-0 (hardcover)
    1. Human cloning—Juvenile literature. [1. Cloning. 2. Genetic
engineering.] I. Title. II. Series.
QH442.2 .G66 2002
174'.25—dc21

                                  2002005702

Printed in the United States of America

10 9 8 7 6 5 4 3 2 1

Illustration Credits: AP/Wide World: pp. 1, 6, 8, 14, 44; Scott
Bauer/U.S. Department of Agriculture, ARS Photo Unit, p. 19; Dr. Jeremy
Burgess/Science Photo Library, p. 36; Corel Corporation, pp. 39, 42;
DíAMAR Interactive Corp., p. 34; Peggy Greb, U.S. Department of
Agriculture, ARS Photo Unit, p. 48; Professors P.M. Motta and J. Van
Blerkom/Science Photo Library, p. 24; Dr. Yorgos Nikas/Science Photo
Library, p. 55; Novisti/Science Photo Library, p. 13; Gary Parker/Science
Photo Library, p. 17; Volker Steger/Science Photo Library, p. 11; U.S.
Department of Energy Human Genome Program, p. 21; Keith
Weller/U.S. Department of Agriculture, ARS Photo Unit, pp. 31, 51.

Cover Illustration: Bluestone/Science Photo Library.

Contents

Chapter 1

The Cloning Debate

On November 25, 2001, a small scientific medical company in Massachusetts called Advanced Cell Technology (ACT) announced that it had cloned a human embryo. The announcement shocked medical researchers and scientists throughout the world. An embryo is the earliest stage of an organism before it has begun to develop into its final form. In the case of a human embryo, this final form will be that of a child. Cloning is the asexual, meaning nonsexual, method of reproducing, or copying, another organism's basic structure. Since this basic structure begins with the formation of an embryo, the Massachusetts company's achievement could be viewed as an important step in the cloning of a human being.[1]

ACT's announcement started another round of debate as to the rightness or wrongness of human cloning that had started nearly twenty-five years previously. In 1978, a science writer named David Rorvik wrote a book called *In His Image: The Cloning of a Man*, in which he claimed that he had witnessed the cloning of a human being. The book was later proven to be a hoax, published appropriately enough the day before April Fool's Day.[2] But the stir created by this hoax was nothing compared to the uproar that followed the announcement

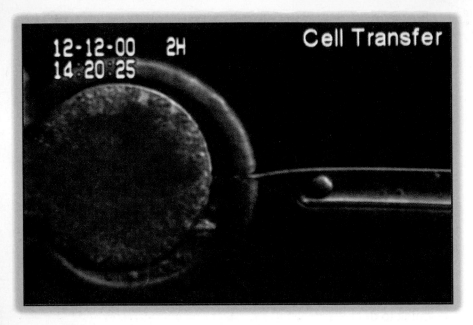

*T*his is a photo of a mammalian cell being injected with DNA during research at Advanced Cell Technology, the company that announced in November 2001 that it had cloned a human embryo.

in February 1997 that scientists in Scotland had successfully cloned a large mammal.

Hello, Dolly!

"SEND IN THE CLONES," "THERE'LL NEVER BE AN UDDER EWE," "A CLONE AGAIN, NATURALLY," "IS CLONING BAAAAAD?"—these were just a few of the headlines that appeared around the world after the news was announced that a team of British scientists had successfully reproduced a lamb, called Dolly, from another, older female sheep. *The New York Times*, which first broke the story in the United States, took a more serious view: "SCIENTIST REPORTS FIRST CLONING EVER OF ADULT MAMMAL" was its headline for its front-page story on February 23, 1997. In smaller type it said, "Feat Is Shock to Experts," and then followed with,

"In Creating Lamb, Researcher Sees Benefits for Medicine, but Others Fear Abuse."[3] That just about summed up the reaction of most readers, if they thought about it at all. Two words stand out here: "shock" and "fear."

The general reaction to the news of Dolly's existence, however, was one of amusement and curiosity. Crowds of newspaper, radio, and television reporters and commentators flocked to the small village of Roslin, Scotland, near the Scottish capital of Edinburgh. When they asked the shepherd tending the large flock of sheep kept at the institute where Dolly had been born, they were delighted to be told that she was easy to recognize because she seemed more lively and curious than the other sheep.[4] Indeed, Dolly trotted up to get a closer look at the reporters and their equipment. The media were quick to decide that Dolly was strictly show business, and this was reinforced when it was learned that Dolly had been named after the country-western singing star Dolly Parton. Dolly was suddenly an international celebrity. She became the subject of countless newspaper and magazine articles, jokes by stand-up comedians, and a symbol of the excellence of modern science. Few reporters could resist referring to the title song of the popular Broadway musical *Hello, Dolly!* when writing their stories. One television reporter attempted to jump into the pen where the sheep were kept in order to be photographed with her arms around the friendly Dolly.[5]

The humorous and curious approach to the Dolly story soon turned more serious when commentators pointed out that if a sheep could be cloned from another sheep, the cloning of a human might be possible. References to popular fiction, movies, and folk tales were made in connection with the experiments at Roslin Institute. Doctor Frankenstein, the fictional scientist who created a monster that soon turned on him with tragic results, was mentioned frequently, along with science-fiction creatures that populated such movies as *Blade*

A sheep named Dolly was the world's first clone of an adult mammal. The cloning technique used to create Dolly was developed by scientists at Roslin Institute in Edinburgh, Scotland.

Runner. In almost all cases, the clones were associated with evil or were considered dangerous. These were not mere robots under the control of human beings, but living creatures with their own needs and desires. The image of their creators put forward by the media was of mad scientists bent on mischief that could only change and endanger our present society.

To the people who had successfully cloned Dolly, the attention and the controversy that arose after the announcement of their achievement came as a surprise. To Ian Wilmut and Keith Campbell, the two scientists who had created Dolly, cloning was nothing new. They had already successfully cloned two sheep using a different method from the one used to clone Dolly, and they certainly did not consider themselves pioneers in the field. Cloning had been part of research in reproduction and heredity for years. Their article in the scientific journal *Nature*, published on February 17, 1997, was entitled "Viable Offspring Derived from Fetal and Adult Mammalian Cells." The unexciting title, however, fooled no one. The important word was "viable," meaning "living," and science writers and editors recognized the article as one of the greatest news stories of the ending of the old century and the beginning of the new.

Dr. Ian Wilmut is an embryologist, a scientist whose area of study is the formation and growth of the embryos of organisms. An *embryo* is the earliest stage of an organism that is under development in an egg or in the womb before its emergence into the world. It begins with the fertilization of an egg by a male reproductive cell called a sperm. The sperm and the egg together make up a single cell called a *zygote*. The zygote then divides into two identical cells called *blastomeres*. The blastomeres divide again into four cells, and then again into eight cells, which is the beginning of the embryo stage. Further division takes place, and the sixteen-cell embryo is now large enough to be visible without the aid of a microscope. About four days after the fertilization of the cell by the sperm, the outer cells of the embryo flatten to become the covering of the embryo called the placenta, and the inner cells become the embryo itself. The whole group of cells now resembles a balloon filled with fluid and is called a *blastocyst*. At around the sixth day, the blastocyst contains 120 cells and begins to attach itself to the uterus, or womb, of the mother, where it connects with the mother's bloodstream. By the fourteenth day, the inner cells of the blastocyst begin to divide rapidly, giving the embryo a head and a tail and a right side and a left side. The cells begin to differentiate, which means that they change their form to take on the tasks of forming the different organs of the body. The embryo has become a *fetus* and will gradually take on the form of the infant that will be delivered at birth.[6]

Roslin Institute

Dr. Wilmut was the head of a team of scientists at Roslin Institute studying the possibility of transferring human genes into sheep with the goal of producing milk with medicinal properties. Dr. Keith Campbell is a cell biologist who studied the growth and changes in the cells of organisms. Together they had the experience and knowledge that led them to the successful cloning of Dolly and other sheep.

Roslin Institute had its beginning in the early part of the twentieth century, when the British government set up a commission to study ways of improving the country's agriculture. Research laboratories were established in various parts of Great Britain. One such laboratory was built in Roslin, Scotland, where it was in close contact with nearby Edinburgh University. This university had long been known for its work in medicine and genetics, the study of genes and heredity. Also located nearby was a small Scottish company called PPL (Pharmaceutical Proteins, Limited) Therapeutics, which was interested in producing drugs from animals to treat human diseases. PPL provided some of the funds and all of the frozen sheep cells that were used in the research that led to the birth of Dolly.[7]

The Debate Begins

Dolly was now a celebrity, and Roslin Institute was gaining recognition as one of the great research centers in the

*I*an Wilmut of Roslin Institute is an embryologist. He and Keith Campbell, a cell biologist, headed the research team that created the first clone of an adult sheep in 1997.

world. As the weeks passed and the media attention became focused on other events, the interest in Dolly and cloning shifted to their meaning for the good of humanity. Dolly's appearance presented a whole series of problems for the world's scientists, politicians, philosophers, and theologians. They were confronted with the possibility that the laboratory process that produced Dolly might work just as well for human beings. The rightness or wrongness of human cloning now became the issue that many political, religious, and scientific leaders realized must be faced.

An international debate began that quickly caught the attention of governments and organizations concerned with human rights. In Europe, most nations had quickly moved to ban human cloning after the birth of Dolly was announced,[8] and their spokespersons urged other nations to do the same or at least justify their positions. The Roman Catholic Church was absolutely opposed to any human meddling with embryos or fetuses and called for a worldwide ban on cloning and any other experiments in reproduction. President Bill Clinton had recently appointed a National Bioethics Advisory Commission (NBAC) to look into the problems that were arising in medical research that uses human subjects. He quickly instructed the NBAC to "conduct a thorough review of the legal and the ethical issues" raised by human cloning. He also ordered that no federal funds be spent on cloning.[9] A week after the president's order, the House of Representatives held hearings on cloning. The Senate followed with their own hearings, which featured the appearance of Dr. Wilmut himself, who was attending a medical conference in Baltimore. Dr. Wilmut repeated his view that human cloning was wrong and had no part in his research. Dr. Wilmut, from the start, had made his views known, and he had been disturbed by some of the reactions to the news of Dolly's birth. What particularly worried him was that many people had written to the institute pleading for the cloning of dying or recently dead relatives and friends. He later told an audience at a public meeting discussing cloning that when it came to cloning another person: "I don't find it frightening. I find it sad."[10] The United States senators received him warmly. One of them told him, "I think you are one of the true trailblazers in human history." Another summed up the feelings of the Senate by saying, "Here we seem to be entering the genetic age."[11]

A researcher at a livestock breeding center in Russia holds cloned rabbits. Although most countries ban human cloning, research into animal cloning has continued.

The Commission's Report

On June 9, 1997, the NBAC published its report to the president, called "Cloning Human Beings." It concluded: "At this time it is morally unacceptable for anyone in the public or private sector, whether in research or clinical setting, to attempt to create a child" using the techniques developed by Dr. Wilmut and his colleagues. President Clinton followed by recommending a law to halt for five years any research toward cloning to create a human being and to cut off federal funds for any such research.[12]

Private Interests

That seemed to settle it as far as the United States government was concerned, but private business interests soon announced that they were ready and able to provide cloning services to the public. One of these was the Missplicity project, founded after a Texas couple donated $2.3 million to Texas A&M University in order for scientists to reproduce their pet dog Missy. Others soon followed, and as recently as 2001, *The New York Times* announced that a spiritual group called the Raelians had plans to clone the cells of a recently dead ten-year-old boy whose parents were devastated by their loss. They claimed that they had the laboratories and the doctors needed for a cloning and a group of volunteer women to carry the cloned fetus until birth.[13] Dr. Panayiotis Zavos, of the University of Kentucky, and Severino Antinori, an Italian researcher, announced that they were forming a group of doctors and scientists to clone a human being. That same year, three doctors, one from the United

*D*r. Severino Antinori (left) and Dr. Panayiotis Zavos announced in 2001 that they were planning to clone a human being. Response from the public and the scientific community was generally very negative.

States, one from Italy, and one from Israel, said that they planned to clone children and that nothing that any government could do would stop them. Furthermore, they had more than six hundred infertile couples who were ready to submit to any procedure the doctors required.[14] Obviously, someone was going to try to clone a human being, if they hadn't done so already. The only questions remaining were when and where.

Education on Cloning

Almost from the beginning of research on human reproduction, scientists have warned that cloning is not the exact reproduction of a human being. Everyone who has ever known identical twins knows how different they can be, even though they share the same genes. The clone of a world-famed violinist or pianist could grow up actually disliking music, or the clone of an athlete might have no interest in sports.

The public needed to be educated on the realities of cloning and other seemingly miraculous achievements of biotechnology. Technology is applied science— science that has been put to use in the form of tools and inventions, for example. *Biotechnology* is technology of a biological nature, of which cloning and genetic engineering are the prime examples.[15] A number of popular books, articles, and public discussions have appeared to fill that need for public education. Indeed, with the attention that it has received, biotechnology may characterize the coming century just as nuclear physics characterized the last.

Chapter 2

Cloning

The birth of Dolly was made possible without the aid of a ram, a male sheep. This non-sexual method of reproduction is called cloning. It is the complete reproduction, or copying, of another organism's basic structure. Cloning occurs in nature among many tiny organisms and even in larger ones, such as certain lizards and fish.[1] Identical human twins, for example, are clones of each other, since they both were produced from a single fertilized egg and therefore contained all of the characteristics, or structure, of that zygote. (Fraternal twins and other multiple births are derived from separate eggs contained in the reproductive organs of the mother and fertilized by separate sperm cells of the father.) But identical twins are the result of natural forces and are not the product of some outside influence, such as farmers' attempts to improve their plants or research scientists' experiments in reproduction.

History

Cloning is not new. In fact, it is almost as old as agriculture, one of man's earliest and most successful means of survival. Whenever a farmer or gardener takes a cutting from one plant and places it in a medium, such as earth or water, in which it will grow, he or she has engaged in cloning. The original purpose of cloning was simply to multiply an existing organism without waiting for nature to do the job. Farmers and then experimenters went on to try to make an existing organism better by improving the medium in which it was reproduced or by mixing in elements that would make it stronger, bigger, more resistant to disease, and more likely to survive. These attempts to multiply and improve organisms have come to be called *genetic engineering*.[2] The word *genetic* means "related to or having to do with genes." Genes are some of the smallest parts of each living thing, whether plant or animal. They are groups of chemicals that are contained in each of the billions of cells that make up our bodies. These chemicals control how our bodies grow and function. They determine whether we are tall or

*I*dentical twins are true natural clones, since they have the same DNA.

short, blue-eyed or brown-eyed, blond or brunette or redhead—in short, they determine what we *are*.

What we now call genes were first described by an Austrian monk named Gregor Mendel. He was interested in plants and flowers and how they became different from one another and how they could be changed to become larger or smaller, differently colored, tastier, easier to grow, and all the other things that farmers had been doing for centuries. Beginning in 1865, Mendel began a series of experiments in which he crossbred different flowers by taking the pollen from one type and transferring it to another. This happens in nature, of course, when a bee carries pollen from one flower to another. Mendel, however, took care to note every type of change that occurred when the crossbred plants reproduced. In other words, he was conducting a scientific experiment, from which certain conclusions could be made. He was describing what happened, not how or why it happened.

Mendel decided that the seeds of the new crossbred plants must contain what he called "particles of inheritance." Each plant had a pair of each particle that determined a plant's characteristic, such as tallness or shortness. These pairs of particles were inherited from the separate plants that had produced the new plant— one particle from each plant. He also determined that one of these particles could be *dominant*, or stronger, than the other. The dominant particle would in most cases determine what the plant turned out to look like. The weaker particle did not disappear, however, and could reappear in later generations of the new plant. In other words, particles, or genes as we now call them, determined heredity.

The microscope was probably invented by a Dutch spectacle maker between 1590 and 1610. This device made it possible for scientists to investigate the structure of living things. In 1665, the English scientist Robert Hooke was one of the first men to build a reflecting microscope. He used it to observe the cells of plants.

*I*n his experiments in genetics, Gregor Mendel looked at many different characteristics of plants, including size and shape of seeds.

Much later, in 1831, a Scottish scientist named Robert Brown observed that each of the tiny cells in plant slices contained a small, thicker substance inside. He decided this was the center of the cell and called it the *nucleus*. In 1839, German botanist Matthias Jakob Schleiden and German zoologist Theodor Schwann, working together, recognized fundamental similarities between plant and animal cells. They proposed that all living things are made up of cells. This theory led to further investigation of these tiny building blocks of living organisms. Further research and experimentation proved that the simplest organisms, such as the paramecium or the amoeba, consist of a single cell containing a nucleus. The most complicated organisms, such as mammals, contain groups of cells acting together to carry out all of the different things the body must do in order to live and survive. It was also discovered that all organisms develop and grow by means of cells dividing and duplicating themselves until the organism reaches its full growth.[3]

Cells and DNA

Cells come in many shapes and forms, but the simplest shape is like that of a target, with the nucleus as the bull's-eye. Surrounding the nucleus is a mass called *cytoplasm*. The nucleus contains the genes an individual plant or animal has inherited from its parents. These genes are parts of structures called *chromosomes*. Chromosomes consist of strands of deoxyribonucleic acid, or DNA, tightly coiled into a double helix pattern (which looks something like a spiral staircase). The double helix is supported by protein scaffolding. These strands of DNA carry the pattern or code of the various genes that determine what a cell's function will be. Certain cells will make up the brain, for example, and others will become the liver or some other organ. DNA controls the fate of all living things. It tells cells what to do, and what the cells do determines what a living thing will become—whether it will be an elephant or a mouse.

The Double Helix

The structure of deoxyribonucleic acid—DNA—was discovered by two biologists, James D. Watson, an American, and Francis Crick, an Englishman They built a model of the DNA molecule and announced their discovery to the world in 1953. Watson and Crick described the DNA molecule as a double helix, which looks like a ladder twisted into a coil. The sides of the ladder, composed of sugar and phosphate molecules, are linked by chemical bonds called base pairs (the steps of the ladder). Each base pair is composed of a combination of two of the chemicals adenine, guanine, cytosine, and thymine (A, G, C, and T).

Adenine always pairs with thymine, and guanine always pairs with cytosine. There are three billion of these letters in the genetic makeup of a human being.

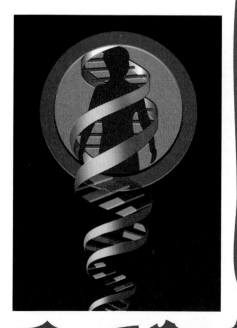

Watson and Crick, along with Maurice H. F. Wilkins, a British biophysicist, received the Nobel Prize in 1962 for their discovery.

Once the working of DNA was understood, scientists felt that they knew enough about cells, genes, and chromosomes that they could start changing them for the better. Suppose, for example, that an individual's DNA code contained a gene that could make him or her susceptible to a disease, such as cancer. It might be possible to remove that gene from the DNA or repair it, thus preventing or treating the disease. Research and experiments along this line led to inventions, instruments, and methods that could remove cells from the body and the nucleus from cells. (A cell with the nucleus removed is called an *enucleated* cell.) They also enabled scientists to remove the nucleus from a cell and replace it with the nucleus from a new cell. This meant that the DNA from the new cell would determine the growth and form of the old cell.

The researchers at Roslin Institute were interested in changing the genes of farm animals to make them more productive, healthier, and a source of drugs that were difficult or costly to produce artificially. They had a variety of animals to work with, and they had isolated cells from many of them. They then stored the cells in freezers for later use in their research. This research proved that the genes of a sheep could be changed so that its milk contained a valuable drug that was used to treat cystic fibrosis, a disease that affects the lungs and makes breathing difficult. The importance of this discovery was obvious not only to doctors but also to drug companies. Sheep could become "drug factories."[4] If a sheep containing this drug could be cloned—that is, reproduced with exactly the same makeup of genes—then there could be hundreds of these drug producers and their offspring working quietly, doing what they had always done—eating and producing milk.

Methods of Cloning

Great advances have been made in the methods of cloning since the role of DNA was discovered in the

1950s. The most common method of cloning is called *molecular cloning*, and it is used to produce medicines such as insulin, which is used to treat diabetes.[5] In this method, pieces of DNA containing genes are placed in a host cell kept in a liquid culture in a petri dish. The cell then divides and produces exact copies of the DNA, which can then be used for experimentation in finding and testing new medicines.

Another method is called *cellular cloning*, in which cells are taken from the body and kept in a liquid culture. The cells divide, producing identical copies of the original. Since this process does not involve egg cells or sperm cells, the cloned cells do not develop any further. This method again provides identical cells for the development of new medicines.[6]

In the 1980s, a much more complicated method of cloning was developed. This was called *nuclear transplantation cloning*. The nucleus of a *somatic*, or body, cell has two sets of genes, one from the father and one from the mother. This is called a *diploid* nucleus. Sperm or egg cells, called *germ cells*, contain only one set of genes. The egg cell contains the mother's genes, and the sperm cell contains the father's genes. The nucleus of a germ cell is called a *haploid* nucleus. In nuclear transplantation cloning, the haploid nucleus of an egg cell is removed, and a diploid nucleus from a somatic cell is put in its place. There is, therefore, only a single genetic parent. This is far different from sexual reproduction, where an egg cell is penetrated by a sperm cell, and the two sets of genes from the egg and sperm cell blend together. The new organism that begins to develop contains a full set of genes from the father and mother. In contrast, the nuclear transplantation clone has only the one set of genes from the diploid nucleus.[7]

In the beginning, nuclear transplantation cloning worked only if the new diploid nucleus introduced into the egg came from an embryo. In the embryonic stage, the dividing cells have not yet become differentiated,

Cell Division

The division of cells is the way an organism grows. There are two types of cell division: asexual, called *mitosis*, and sexual, called *meiosis*.

Mitosis occurs only in somatic, or body, cells. The nucleus of a single somatic cell divides into two daughter nuclei with the same genetic material. Then the cytoplasm divides and the cell splits in two. These two cells divide. All of the cells go on dividing and the organism grows. Dolly was cloned from somatic cells, and mitosis was the process that produced her.

Meiosis occurs after a pair of germ cells—sperm cells from the male and egg cells from the female—unite and form a single cell in the process called fertilization. The nucleus of the new cell contains genetic material from both parents. The nucleus then divides, with each resulting nucleus duplicating the genetic material from the original. The new cells continue to divide and the organism grows. This is the normal way that complicated organisms such as mammals reproduce. (Shown at right are mouse cells viewed through a scanning electron microscope. They are in the early embryonic stage, at about four days after fertilization.)

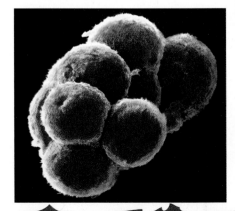

which means that they have not yet been assigned their different functions. In other words, embryonic cells have not yet become hair cells, skin cells, muscle cells, or any other of the cells that make up a complete organism, whether animal or human. For this reason, scientists believed that it would be impossible to clone an organism from a fully formed animal or human whose cells had long since differentiated and had completed their task of forming the body.[8]

The Dolly Method

Nuclear transplantation was the method that Dr. Wilmut and his team of scientists at Roslin Institute used in cloning Dolly. The difference was that the diploid nucleus they introduced into the enucleated egg cell came from an adult sheep. This meant that the nucleus they implanted in the egg was a differentiated nucleus, one that had been given just one function, which in this case was a mammary cell taken from the sheep's udder. How could a complete sheep be produced from a cell that had only one function?

Roslin Institute researchers had already cloned a sheep, called Polly, by the nuclear transplantation method using the usual embryonic cell as the diploid nucleus. They knew that this method worked because the embryonic cell contained all of the genes necessary for the development of a complete sheep and that these cells were active. Once the cell began dividing and developing into a fetus, the later stage of development when the embryo begins to take the form of its animal or human body, most of the genes in a differentiated nucleus would become unnecessary. If a cell was destined to be a muscle cell, those genes that determined nerve cells, bone cells, and the others would be "turned off," or inactive. This "turned-off" state is sometimes called *quiescence* or *hibernation*. Whatever term is used, it means that the other genes in the nucleus are still there, only turned off.[9]

How Dolly Was Cloned

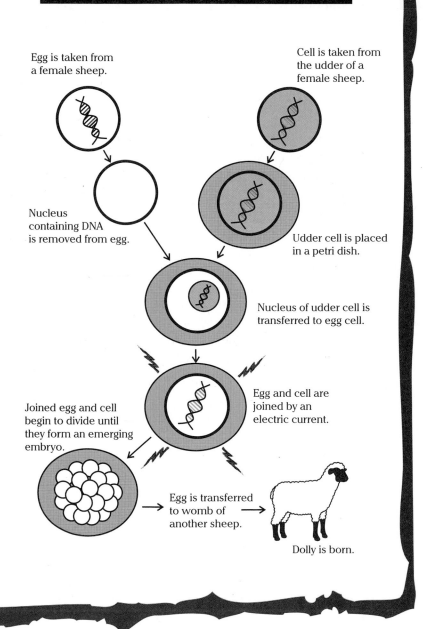

Egg is taken from a female sheep.

Cell is taken from the udder of a female sheep.

Nucleus containing DNA is removed from egg.

Udder cell is placed in a petri dish.

Nucleus of udder cell is transferred to egg cell.

Joined egg and cell begin to divide until they form an emerging embryo.

Egg and cell are joined by an electric current.

Egg is transferred to womb of another sheep.

Dolly is born.

Roslin Institute researchers found a way to awaken these sleeping genes so that they would again become turned on. They took a somatic cell from an adult sheep and deprived it of its nutrients by placing it in a petri dish. They literally starved it, until it also became turned off. They then took the quiescent nucleus and implanted it into an egg that had had its nucleus removed. They then placed the egg with its new nucleus in a nutrient broth and gave it an electric shock. This awakened the nucleus and reactivated not only the differentiated gene but also all of the other genes in the nucleus. They now had what amounted to an embryonic cell that contained all of the genetic information to develop a complete sheep. The electric shock also made the egg believe that it had been fertilized, and it began dividing. What the researchers had done was to wake up all of the genes in an old cell and make it young again, so to speak. It had then "tricked" an egg with a new nucleus into thinking it had been fertilized. After about a week, the researchers transferred what was now an embryo into the womb of another sheep, where it gradually and naturally grew into a fetus and was finally delivered as a baby lamb—Dolly.[10]

When the news of Dolly's birth was presented to the scientific community, Roslin researchers were careful to point out that in their attempts they had joined 277 cells to eggs. Only twenty-nine of these grew into embryos that could be transferred to the womb of another sheep. Thirteen of these were successfully implanted into ewes. Out of these, only Dolly survived as a whole and healthy lamb.[11]

The World Reacts

One of the first reactions to the announcement of Dolly's birth was the thought of using the "Dolly method" to clone a human being. Government, religious, and social organizations and spokespersons were quick to respond to the possibility of human cloning. Many were outraged at what they believed was a threat to the very meaning

How a Human Might Be Cloned

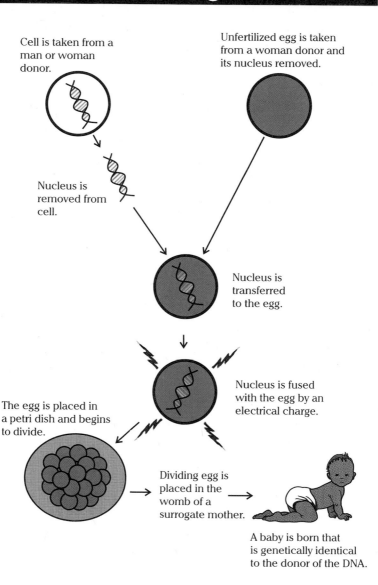

Cell is taken from a man or woman donor.

Unfertilized egg is taken from a woman donor and its nucleus removed.

Nucleus is removed from cell.

Nucleus is transferred to the egg.

Nucleus is fused with the egg by an electrical charge.

The egg is placed in a petri dish and begins to divide.

Dividing egg is placed in the womb of a surrogate mother.

A baby is born that is genetically identical to the donor of the DNA.

of what it is to be human. Human beings are the result of the mixing of two different sets of genes, they argued, and any violation of that most basic fact of human life is outrageous. In March 1997, President Bill Clinton banned the use of federal funds for any research connected with human cloning.[12] He directed the new National Bioethics Advisory Commission to investigate the whole matter of cloning, particularly regarding its ethical and legal aspects. In August 1997, President Clinton proposed legislation banning the cloning of humans for at least five years. In September 1997, over sixty thousand scientists agreed to a five-year waiting period on human cloning. In January 1998, nineteen European countries agreed to ban human cloning. That same month, a scientist from Chicago, Richard Seed, published his intention to perform experiments in human cloning.[13] If he was prevented by law, he said, he would move offshore and clone humans in some other country. On January 20, 1998, the U.S. Food and Drug Administration (FDA) declared its authority to oversee any human cloning experiments, which meant that it would be a criminal offense to attempt any human cell transfer without the FDA's approval.

The controversy was heating up, with just about anyone with access to the media joining in. It has continued to heat up, and came to near boiling point when, in January 2001, three doctors from the United States, Italy, and Israel announced that they planned to clone children.[14] Shortly after that, the English Parliament approved a change in their country's laws to permit the creation of cloned human embryos for use in scientific research. Cracks had begun to appear in the worldwide opposition to human cloning, and it began to appear that it was, as many experts said from the start, bound to happen.[15]

Chapter 3

Why Clone?

When the National Bioethics Advisory Commission submitted its report on human cloning to President Clinton on June 9, 1997, one of the first questions it answered was, Why pursue animal cloning research? The commission gave a concise answer: Research on nuclear transfer cloning in animals may provide information that will be useful in agriculture, medicine, and the growing area of biotechnology.

The commission went on to list the goals of this research:

1. To create groups of animals with identical genes to be used for research purposes.

2. To rapidly increase the number of desirable animals.

3. To make more efficient the production and increase in number of genetically engineered livestock.

4. To produce desired genetic changes in farm animals.

5. To pursue basic knowledge about cell differentiation.[1]

There was no mention of *human* cloning as a goal of

A technician with the U.S. Department of Agriculture reads livestock DNA sequences. Supporters of cloning point out that it is a helpful tool in animal research.

nuclear transfer cloning. The report was generally in favor of animal cloning, and although some animal rights groups objected, the general public seemed to go along with the report. In the meantime, the debate for and against cloning was beginning to take shape, and the basic argument seemed to be over ethics—whether it was right or wrong to clone human beings.

Reasons for Cloning

Leaving aside the commission's favorable goals of cloning in general, the arguments in favor of cloning began to focus on its social aspects and what it could mean to individuals.

Human cloning would allow infertile couples to have children. Married couples who are unable to have children either because of sterility in the male or infertility in the female, or both, could have a child biologically related to them. The cloned child would belong to the parents, with all the privileges and responsibilities of parenthood.[2] Some people believe that cloning would be preferable to adoption. The adoption process is difficult, lengthy, and expensive, while cloning by nuclear transfer would not involve red tape.

Human cloning could eliminate the risk of passing on a hereditary disease. The passing on of hereditary disease can be avoided by substituting sperm or eggs from a healthy donor through such procedures as artificial insemination or in vitro fertilization. Many couples object to this because it introduces a third person's genes in the offspring. Human cloning would give the offspring the genes of one of the parents—and no one else.[3]

Human cloning could provide a twin from which a person could obtain an organ for transplant. Cloning would solve the problem of the body's rejection of an organ transplant. It is often difficult or even impossible to find a transplant donor whose tissue or organ is a perfect match for the person who is receiving the transplant. A transplant from a clone would present no such problem. Of course, the organ to be transplanted would not be one essential to the life of the clone, such as a heart. A cloned twin would be something of an insurance policy against future organic problems. It could be argued that this is an inhuman approach to solving a physical problem. But there have been cases in the past where parents of a child in need of a transplant have conceived another

Assisted Reproduction

Assisted reproduction techniques are used when a natural fertilization and pregnancy are not possible or are not desired.

Artificial insemination (AI). Introduction of male sperm directly into a woman's reproductive tract by injection. If all goes well, the woman undergoes a natural pregnancy and gives birth.

In vitro fertilization (IVF). The fertilization of a woman's egg by bringing her egg and a sperm together outside the body in a petri dish. After cell division takes place, the egg is returned to the mother's womb. The first babies born as a result of this method were called "test-tube babies."

Surrogate motherhood. A surrogate is a deputy or a substitute for someone else. In surrogate motherhood, an embryo produced by IVF is implanted in the womb of another woman. She undergoes pregnancy and delivers a baby that is considered the child of the couple whose egg and sperm produced the embryo.

Cloning. An asexual (nonsexual) method of reproduction stemming from a single cell. It involves the implantation of an embryo produced by the joining of an unfertilized, enucleated egg with an undifferentiated nucleus from another cell. The embryo is then implanted in the original mother or a surrogate mother. This method has not yet been tried on humans, but has been successful with mammals such as sheep and cows.

child in order for that second child to supply the transplant, and the second child has been no less loved and cared for than the first child.[4]

Human cloning could enable people to replace someone who had been dear to them. This possibility has brought much ridicule to the whole idea of cloning, largely because of the number of requests that researchers and experimenters have received for clones of dead or dying pets. But for the grieving parents of the child who has died, cloning might represent a

*M*any couples feel strongly about having children who are genetically related to them.

genuine consolation. However, it would need to be explained to them that they would not be obtaining the lost child but rather a new child with the same genes. If human cloning is possible and made legal, some people might choose this option.[5]

Human cloning could make possible the duplication of people of great genius, talent, character, or other qualities. Again, this idea is based on the confused notion that clones are exact duplicates of the original rather than another person with the same genes. Nevertheless, genes determine special characteristics, and any clone of an artist, athlete, or performer would most likely be capable of at least some achievement in the same field as the cloned individual. The likelihood is strong that some notable person would want to have himself or herself cloned and that it would be done somewhere by a willing scientist.[6]

Animal cloning could help save endangered species or revive extinct species. The novel and movie *Jurassic Park* brought this possibility to light even before Dolly was cloned. Commentators were quick to point out, however, that this was fiction and could not happen. In order for cloning to be successful, the DNA transferred must be active, and this was not the case in the prehistoric creatures featured in the film. But with recent advances in cloning techniques, reviving recently extinct species or saving endangered species has become not only a possibility but a reality.

A gaur is an oxlike animal native to southeastern Asia. Its population has been reduced to fewer than 36,000, and the gaur is in danger of becoming lost to the world. In 1997, researchers from Advanced Cell Technology collected skin cells from a gaur that had recently died. The researchers then extracted eggs from dairy cows that had recently died and removed the nucleus from them. They then injected a gaur cell with its nucleus containing DNA into the cow eggs. An electric shock was then passed through the eggs, and the eggs and nucleus merged. The eggs began to divide, and when a sufficient mass had developed, the researchers implanted them into healthy cows. Out of 692 injected cells, 81 grew sufficiently to be implanted in cows. Forty-four were implanted in cows, and out of these, one survived. These numbers were better than those used in cloning Dolly.[7] Noah, as the new gaur was called, later died, but the researchers insist the cause was infection rather than birth defects. That Noah was born at all represented "an important milestone," according to Dr. Ian Wilmut.[8]

Cloning of humans and animals is necessary for the advancement of science. This is perhaps the most widely and most strongly held argument for continuing the

*A*dvocates of cloning say that it could be used to revive extinct species. Shown is an engraving of a dodo, a flightless bird related to the pigeon, which became extinct around 1760.

cloning of mammals. If we halt this research, scientists say, it would be a backward step not only for science but for all of humankind. Without citing the benefits to be gained by cellular research, which includes cloning, they speak in general terms of the advancement of human knowledge and well-being. This position was perhaps best summed up by the U.S. senator from Iowa, Tom Harkin. Early in the debate, in 1998, he declared, "I do not think there are any appropriate limits to human knowledge."[9] The past is filled with examples of attempts by kings, clergy, governments, and social groups to halt the progress of new ideas in science. Almost all of these previously scorned ideas and developments have proved beneficial to mankind. At one time, artificial insemination was banned. X rays were considered little more than witchcraft, test-tube babies and in vitro fertilization were scorned as unnatural and evil, and organ transplants were thought of as an insult to nature and humanity.[10] To those who say that cloning research is demeaning to human nature, Senator Harkin replies: "I think that any attempt to limit the pursuit of human knowledge is demeaning to human nature."[11]

Some religious groups approve of cloning. Except for the Catholic Church and some conservative Protestant denominations, the religious stand on cloning has been roughly the same as that of the Advisory Commission: cautious but aware of the good that could result from it and in favor of continued research so long as it is safe. An Orthodox Jewish rabbi told the committee that the Jewish tradition holds that humans should help to master the world as long as they do not go against God's will. He claimed that it would not be in the Jewish character to go against a technology that might do good or to decide not to use it before it has been proven that it is not useful.[12] Nancy Duff, a Protestant theologian, said that cloning might be either a miracle given by God or another attempt by humans to play at creation, and, at the very least, any attempt to ban it should be put on hold until all the evidence is in.[13]

Acceptance or endorsement of cloning by religious groups seems rather subdued compared to the outright and forceful opposition to cloning expressed by religious groups that oppose it.

Chapter 4

Why Not to Clone

When the idea of cloning left the pages of science fiction and entered the mainstream of public awareness, public reaction was mostly negative. And when the possibility of cloning humans was suggested, opinions became much more heated and the warnings against it much more forceful. Animal rights groups came out against cloning and all other experiments on animals simply because they considered it cruel and the animals themselves had no choice in the matter.[1] Religious leaders opposed it because to them it was an indication that experimenters were "playing God" and had no right to create what might turn out to be "soulless creatures."[2] Some biologists and other scientists were against cloning, particularly human cloning, because clones are genetic duplicates of only one parent and can pass on any faulty genes to their descendants; there is no chance of genetic improvement or avoidance, as in two-parent offspring.[3] Just about every special-interest group entered the debate, and the overwhelming feeling seemed to be that cloning, especially human cloning, was undesirable and not in the public interest.

In 1998, the National Bioethics Advisory Commission stated that "at this time it is morally unacceptable for anyone in the public or private sector, whether in a research or clinical setting, to attempt to create a child using somatic nuclear transfer cloning."[4] In addition to considering scientific, religious, and social objections to human cloning, the commission listed four issues that it considered in making its decisions: (1) individuality and freedom of the will, (2) family integrity, (3) treating children as objects, and (4) safety.[5]

The commission was well aware from testimony by experts that a human clone would not be an exact copy of another person but would develop in its environment just as an identical twin would. And yet they believed that a human clone would feel that his or her very life had been determined by forces that were not natural. He or she would somehow feel robbed of a life that other

*T*he idea of cloning a much-loved family pet has brought ridicule to the whole concept of cloning.

people come by naturally. Clones would feel that their future was not determined by their own choices. Cloning would violate an individual's "unique identity."[6]

The commission also heard testimony that cloning violates "the essential reality of the human family."[7] Most people take their identity or form their opinions of themselves from a network of living parents and relatives and generations of forebears. Most adopted children or children born as a result of artificial insemination do not feel estranged from the family they have been placed with. But in many cases, when they reach adulthood, they search keenly for their biological parents. A cloned child might very well be cut off from this close kinship, and the other members of the family themselves might feel estranged from this newcomer in their midst.

A third concern of the commission was what they called the "objectification" of clones.[8] This, they thought, would mean treating children as if they were no more than objects. For example, if a clone-child is produced in order to provide an organ transplant for the original child who is dangerously ill, it could rob the clone-child of any dignity. He or she could be treated merely as a means to an end, with possible psychological damage.

On the matter of safety, the commission's concern was much simpler. It took many attempts at nuclear transfer, and the loss of many embryos, to produce one living sheep. The question is, Should we be ready to accept such uncertainty and risks to produce what might also be a human being that was not completely healthy or whole? Even if a successful birth is achieved, there is no guarantee that some damage or condition in the nuclear transfer has not altered the genes or changed the genetic code, which could result in later physical or mental problems.

Reasons We Should Not Clone

Most commentators agree that there is some physical risk in cloning, but they are divided on the social and psychological effects of the procedure. Again, on this issue, the opponents of human cloning appear to outnumber the supporters.

Cloning is inhuman. Since the dawn of humanity, the reproductive act has determined the fate of the human species. Humans are nothing without forebears, who combined to produce the species over centuries and uncounted generations. The majority of people can no more think of themselves as evolving in a test tube or a petri dish than they can imagine coming from outer space borne as a spore or a virus on a meteor. Until now. If human cloning becomes possible and legal, it would take away that feeling of continuity and confidence that results from belonging to a huge family of like individuals springing from a common experience. The clone would be outside that experience and therefore might be considered less than human.[9]

Cloning could mean the end of sexual reproduction. Shortly after the announcement of the cloning of Dolly and the raising of the possibility of cloning humans, *The New York Times* quoted a woman biologist as saying that if cloning were easily accomplished, "there'd be no need for men."[10] She was joking, but many have taken the possibility seriously. If human cloning became possible, a woman could produce a clone without a man. All that would be required, besides the cloning techniques, would be DNA, an egg, and a womb, either her own or another woman's.

Objections to the idea of cloning as a replacement for sexual reproduction have been overwhelming. The chief objection has been that it would take away the advantages of breeding. The mingling of genes has been the means whereby the human species has developed resistance to various germs, viruses, diseases, and other enemies of our physical makeup.[11] Having only one set of genes, or closely related genes, lowers our resistance to these invaders of our systems and leaves us open to infection and disease. Artificial insemination, in vitro fertilization, and surrogate motherhood have been developed to overcome the inability to breed, not to reduce the importance of sex as a means of reproduction.

Human cloning could cause psychological damage to the clone. Although the possibility of psychological damage to clones has been touched on by the NBAC, other commentators had much more to say. Clones would certainly be aware of their natural predecessors and might suppose that their life course would be the same. This could discourage any ambition or hopes that they might have. Or clones might feel expected to match the accomplishments, if any, of the cloned persons. In

*S*ome people have pointed out that cloning could be detrimental because a clone would be expected to have the same achievements as the original. For instance, a clone of a great musician would also be expected to be musically gifted.

any case, their pride or satisfaction in their life direction could be diminished. Any sense of individuality, specialness, or freedom could be lost, and this—combined with the pressures of expectations—could cause severe psychological damage.[12]

Human cloning would present grave risks to the clone. Possible risks to the clone were touched on by the NBAC and elaborated on by later critics of cloning. In addition to the possibility of mistakes or accidents in the cloning process, there are other dangers to take into account. For one, the adult cell that was transferred to the egg cell may have picked up mutations over the course of the donor's life, including an openness to a disease such as cancer or diabetes, which could be passed on to the clone. Also, the whole experimental process involves trial and error. If an error is made and an imperfect specimen is the result, the specimen is disposed of. In human cloning, the error may not show up for months or even years. It would be heartless, as well as criminal, to dispose of an imperfect clone that had survived the rigors of birth.[13]

All of the arguments in favor of human cloning have made the assumption that it is possible and safe. Cloning opponents argue that the focus of the debate has been on ethical and moral issues. They say not enough thought has been given to the actual physical dangers in cloning, both in the process itself and in the end result, which could be flawed. This argument was given strong support when it was discovered in January 2002 that Dolly, the first successful and apparently healthy cloned mammal, had developed arthritis, a bone disease that can be extremely painful as well as crippling. Dr. Ian Wilmut, Dolly's creator, himself admitted that "this provides one more piece of evidence that, unfortunately, the present cloning procedures are rather inefficient."[14]

Human cloning could be used for commercial purposes. In 1998, an Australian firm called Southern Cross Genetics was formed with the purpose of preserving DNA

*T*he first cloned cat was named "cc" (for "carbon copy"). While she appeared healthy and frisky, some animal clones have had health problems.

for future cloning. Graeme Sloan, the firm's founder, said, "I don't have a scientific background. I'm pure business. I'd be lying if I said I wasn't here to make a dollar out of it."[15] He went on to say that there is a fortune to be made, and everyone is racing to get in on it. He later sold his firm to a French company and then disappeared. For many critics of cloning, this outright commercialism is one of the worst possibilities. They envision a supermarket for DNA, or a "dial-a-clone" operation in which customers specify the type of child they want. This possibility sums up many of the objections to human cloning: the demeaning of human life, the objectification of children, the loss of identity, and the risks involved, which could only increase as mass production took over.

Human cloning has been banned in many countries and at least five U.S. states,[16] and the pressure from anti-cloning groups for a worldwide ban has increased due to the cloning of a human embryo in November 2001. Even if such a ban were imposed, underground factories could still exist, but the operators and their customers would be at risk of exposure and punishment.

Human cloning could be used by governments or groups to further their own interests or goals. The possible use of human cloning by governments or groups to further their own interests is one of the darkest sides of human cloning. It has been used as the subject or plot of many science-fiction novels and motion pictures. Clones as slaves, clones as robotlike servants, clones as uncomplaining laborers in horrifying working conditions, clo⎽ ⎽⎽⎽⎽ ⎽inea pigs in dangerous experiments, be sacrificed when required—these ⎽possibilities for the misuse of human

⎽n cloning could make possible the creation of a ⎽r race. The idea of racial superiority has plagued ⎽ankind almost from the beginnings of human history. Primitive tribes' names for themselves usually translate as "human beings," meaning that they see all those outside the tribe as not human. As recently as the 1930s and 1940s, the idea of a master race was one of the causes of a war that caused massive destruction and loss of life. The idea of "ethnic cleansing" is still alive in the Balkans and Africa. The foes of human cloning claim that nuclear transfer makes it possible to create people with what the creators consider desirable characteristics. For instance, it would be possible for a dictator to direct his scientists to clone only those of his party, or his race, or even his hair color. This possibility has been brought to the attention of a wide public through science-fiction books and movies. In one book that was made into a movie, *The Boys from Brazil*, a scientist clones identical Hitlers from cells preserved from the dead dictator. In another movie, *Sleeper*, a comic approach to the same subject, a dictator's nose is to be preserved for later cloning. In another, *Gattaca*, a whole society is dominated by a privileged few who have been genetically selected. The possibility of this happening might seem far-fetched, but the continuation of the idea makes it potentially dangerous or destructive.[18]

Human cloning could be used to solve social problems. Some commentators have suggested that many social problems are due to genetic differences among people.[19] They claim that the inequalities that exist among races, nationalities, and economic classes are the result of faulty genes rather than environmental, economic, or oppressive forces. They even blame criminal tendencies on genes that are somehow different

A Cloning Hoax

On March 31, 1978, the day before April Fool's Day, a book titled *In His Image: The Cloning of a Man* was published by a respected American publisher. It was written by a freelance science writer named David Rorvik, who claimed that he had helped a billionaire have himself cloned. According to Rorvik, the billionaire contacted him because he admired Rorvik's writing and asked him to put him in touch with a scientist who would be willing to carry out the experiment. For this service he would pay one million dollars. Rorvik eventually found a scientist, and together they found egg donors and a woman who was willing to act as the surrogate into whom the cloned embryo would be implanted. The baby was born just before Christmas 1976, two years before the first in vitro fertilization and decades after scientists had been trying to clone frogs and mice.

Scientists everywhere were outraged that such a claim could be made. The story made sensational headlines, and commentators criticized the experiment, if true, as another example of science gone out of control. Public fears of mad scientists creating monsters and mindless slaves were encouraged by articles in newspapers and magazines. Public concern became so great that a congressional hearing was held at which many important scientists testified that the book was a hoax and that human cloning was impossible. The book was eventually exposed as untrue, but not before many distinguished scientists had gone on record as stating that cloning a mammal, particularly from adult cells, was impossible. With the cloning of Dolly, they were proved wrong.

Source: Gina Kolata, *Clone: The Road to Dolly and the Path Ahead* (New York: William Morrow and Company, Inc., 1998), pp. 93–119.

from those of law-abiding citizens. In cloning, they claim, these faulty genes could be removed from the nucleus or otherwise rendered harmless before they are implanted in the receiver eggs. Such a scheme could be compared to brainwashing, by which those in power can control those who disagree with or oppose them. The scientific evidence that social problems are the result of bad genes is slight if not nonexistent, but the idea could be attractive to anyone bent on changing or "improving" society.[20]

Some religious groups disapprove of cloning. When it became apparent that the cloning of human beings was possible, religious leaders of most faiths issued warnings about the danger of "playing God." The strongest Christian opposition so far has come from the Roman Catholic Church. In 1987, long before the creation of Dolly, spokesmen for the Church in the Vatican absolutely condemned cloning and all other technical methods of reproduction (such as artificial insemination and in vitro fertilization). After the cloning of Dolly, the Vatican called for a worldwide movement to ban cloning. One of the Church's objections is that human beings have been given knowledge and free will so that they can search for and recognize the true and the good. Cloning would go beyond that gift. Humans were not given "the power to alter their nature or the manner in which they came into existence."[21] Southern Baptist and United Methodist leaders seem to go along with this view, and have adopted resolutions against human cloning.[22]

The Catholic Church's position on cloning is in line with its position on abortion, and it admits no circumstances in which either would be acceptable. Islam, which does not have a definite center such as Roman Catholicism has in the Vatican, has not yet made a clear-cut judgment on cloning. But one of its strict fundamentalist branches, the Shiite, has left no doubt about how it feels. One of its legal scholars has suggested that anyone who clones a human being should be executed.[23] The spokespersons for most other religions,

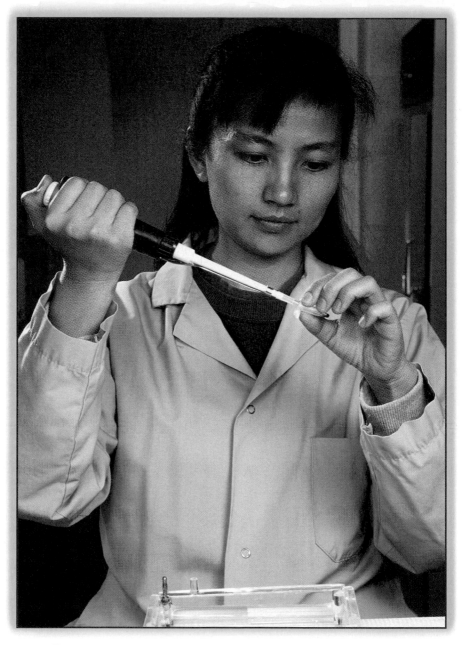

*O*pponents of human cloning argue that science has not taken into account the ills that it might bring. Above, a researcher prepares a sample for gene screening.

however, while warning of cloning's possible negative effects on marriage, the family, human identity, and dignity, believe that cloning could be beneficial. However, it would first have to be proved that cloning was safe for all who took part in the cloning process. But these people also feel that it should be strictly regulated and kept under social or governmental control.

Except for the Roman Catholic Church and some conservative Protestant denominations, there does not seem to be any firm religious stand for or against cloning. Some commentators believe, however, that if there is a gradual public acceptance of cloning and the easing of government or social restrictions on it, the religious opposition from the Catholic Church and fundamentalists might be the only one that remains.

Chapter 5

Brave New World

> O brave new world,
> That has such people in't!
> —Shakespeare, *The Tempest*,
> Act V, Scene 1

Many books and articles on cloning and the new fields of biotechnology and genetic engineering have used this phrase from Shakespeare in their titles or subtitles. The first of these was the novel *Brave New World* by Aldous Huxley, which was published in 1932. In it he imagined a world in which clones were used to fill undesirable social roles. They were little more than robotlike slaves doing menial tasks to support a more intelligent and privileged class. This brave new world would be achieved through advances in what the cloners of Dolly have called "biological control."[1] This phrase embraces all of genetic research and its offshoots, including cloning. Biological control, scientists claim, promises great benefits to humankind.

Cloning of farm animals in order to improve the breeds or increase their productivity is now commonplace. Cyagra, a Massachusetts company, is now cloning prize breeding cows and says that its methods may become an easy and cheap way to produce dairy and meat animals.[2] Cloning of certain animals such as the pig, some of whose organs can be accepted by the human body without rejection, has advanced beyond the research stage and may soon become an important source of scarce organs for transplants.[3]

The Human Genome Project

The Human Genome Project, which began in the 1980s, is a worldwide effort by scientists to find the entire DNA sequence, or lineup, of the human genome. The genome is the complete set of instructions, sometimes called a code, for the growth and activity of every cell in an organism. This code is found in every nucleus of every living cell. Genes give the directions for the production of protein, the basic building block of all living tissue. How

*C*loning has been proposed as an easy way to produce animals for meat and dairy products and even replacement organs for human beings.

genes produce protein is a complicated process, but it depends on the combination four different chemical bases: adenine, guanine, cytosine, and thymine, or A, G, C, and T. The different combinations of these bases make up the code by which protein is instructed to take its various forms and develop into different functions. The double helix is packaged into a structure known as a chromosome. Each cell normally contains twenty-three pairs of chromosomes, one inherited from each parent, including one unmatched pair called X and Y. The X and Y chromosomes determine whether a person is male or female. (Women have two X chromosomes; men have an X and a Y.)

The Ten Best Movies About Cloning

Hollywood producers have always liked the unnatural creation of life, which, for them, most often resulted in monsters. Many of these movies are not really about cloning, but rather genetic engineering, but the idea is the same. Here is a chronological list of the top ten:

Invasion of the Body Snatchers (1956). Citizens of a small town are somehow cloned when strange pods are placed beside them when they sleep. Their clones turn out to be robotlike creatures who want to take over the world.

Sleeper (1973). In this comedy, followers of a dictator intend to clone their leader from all that his left of him after his death—his nose.

The Boys From Brazil (1978). Former Nazi official Dr. Josef Mengele, who has escaped to Brazil, clones boys from samples of skin and blood taken from Adolf Hitler before his death.

Blade Runner (1982). Clones, here called androids, have mutinied in their colonies in outer space and have made their way to Earth, which they intend to take over.

The objective of the Human Genome Project was to map the different combinations of A, G, C, and T for the entire human genome. Two groups, one public and one private, competed to decipher the code, making it into as much a race as a scientific endeavor. The competition did, however, speed up the research and experimentation. On February 15, 2001, the two groups, the National Genome Research Institute and the Celera Genomics Group, together announced that the genetic code had been broken and claimed that the achievement represented "a pinnacle of human self-knowledge."[4]

One of the main advantages of knowing the sequence or placement of genes is the ability to identify

Terminator 2 (1991). A futuristic clone, here called a cyborg, returns to the present to protect a benefactor of mankind whose death would undo all the good he can do for the world. He is opposed by an evil clone.

Jurassic Park (1993). A billionaire clones dinosaurs to stock an island theme park. The creatures threaten to take over the island.

Species (1995). Scientists tampering with DNA experiments clone a monster that takes the form of a beautiful woman, who creates havoc.

Multiplicity (1996). An overworked construction worker tries to solve his problems by having himself cloned. His three clones turn out to have different personalities and work habits.

Gattaca (1997). In the future, well-to-do parents can have all imperfections removed from their children by genetic engineering, which leads to rigid social class structure.

Austin Powers: The Spy Who Shagged Me (1999). In this spoof of 1960s spy films, the villain, Dr. Evil, has had himself cloned. Dr. Evil calls the clone Mini-Me.

any genes that may cause an inheritable disease. Knowing the gene and where it is located will enable scientists to study its nature and perhaps alter its effects through therapies or even removal. Cloning would be an important part of these new developments and techniques. The transferred nucleus could be tinkered with before it is inserted into the enucleated egg. The social problems that could arise are fairly clear. After all, if you know the complete sequence of the donor's DNA, you might as well get rid of those traits that you or society might consider undesirable. This would be nothing less than human engineering, that much-debated aspect of human cloning. On the other hand, if you can identify the genes that may cause epilepsy, drug addiction, brain damage, and other disorders, it gives scientists the opportunity to study them for the purpose of replacing or altering them to render them harmless. From all of this may come new treatments and new drugs, and the potential for profits to be gained from them is as great as the benefits to society.

Stem Cell Research and Therapeutic Cloning

So far, human cloning has been banned or is about to be banned in Britain, Canada, Japan, Portugal, Germany, and France. In January 2001, the Council of Europe, an organization created after World War II to unite European countries, proposed a ban on human cloning. Twenty-four European countries have signed the treaty, and five have ratified it.[5]

The treaty is careful to separate stem cell research and the cloning of embryos from human cloning. An embryo is a group of stem cells, which are cells that have not yet become differentiated to form the different types of cells that make up an organism. By extracting the stem cells from the embryo, scientists can direct their growth in a lab to become differentiated cells that could take the place of damaged or faulty cells in an organism. Diseases, physical disorders, or injuries that result from cell damage or failure could be cured by the injection of healthy cells that have been differentiated to make the type of cell that is needed.[6]

Also in January 2001, the government of Great Britain, which has forcefully opposed cloning from the beginning, announced that it would approve "therapeutic cloning" of embryos up to fourteen days old.[7] Therapeutic cloning means the use of cloning techniques for medical purposes only, not for reproduction. The embryos used in this type of cloning will supply stem cells that will be used in research to combat illnesses such as Alzheimer's disease, Parkinson's disease, cancer, and diabetes.

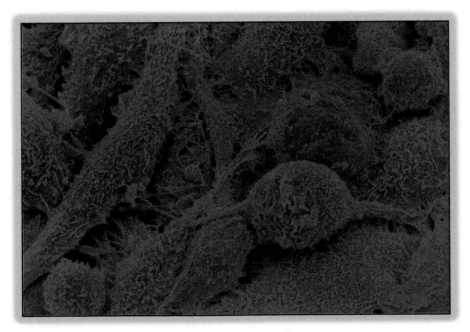

*S*hown are mammalian stem cells—cells formed shortly after fertilization that have not yet become differentiated to perform particular functions. Scientists hope that stem cell research will eventually lead to treatment for disease and injury.

After a long debate, in July 2001 the United States House of Representatives passed a bill banning all forms of human cloning, including the cloning of human embryos for purposes of stem cell research. But in June 2002, the U.S. Senate rejected the bill, despite its backing by President George W. Bush, and it appears to have little chance of revival in its present form. Although President Bush has supported a total ban on human cloning, he is still considering the use of government funds to support stem cell research using noncloned human embryos left over from use for in vitro fertilization.[8] In late November 2001, the European Parliament rejected a proposed ban on human embryo cloning in the European Union (EU). This acceptance of human embryo cloning was largely symbolic, however, since each member nation of the EU would have to pass its own legislation on the matter.[9]

The Future of Cloning

Human cloning could be a part of the advance in genetic engineering, but it is not essential to it. It is, however, tempting to businesspeople as well as scientists, and to the adventurous as well as the merely curious. Richard Seed, the Chicago scientist who has vowed to clone a human being no matter what, has said: "The first person to produce a healthy human clone will be the winner of the Super Bowl."[10] One thing is certain: Whoever achieves it will undoubtedly become either famous or notorious, depending on your outlook. But, as many observers have commented, it is not a question of who will do it, or how it will be done, but when it will be done. Some suggest that it may have been attempted already, but there will be no announcement of it until it has been proven successful.[11]

Chapter 1. The Cloning Debate

1. Jose B. Cibelli, Robert P. Lanza, and Michael D. West, "The First Human Cloned Embryo," *Scientific American*, November 24, 2001, <http://www.sciam.com/explorations/2001/112401> (November 25, 2001).

2. Gina Kolata, *Clone: The Road to Dolly and the Path Ahead* (New York: William Morrow and Company, Inc., 1998), p. 93.

3. Gina Kolata, "Scientist Reports First Cloning Ever of Adult Mammal," *The New York Times*, February 23, 1997, p. A1.

4. Charles Siebert, "An Audience With Dolly," *The New York Times Magazine*, September 24, 2000, p. 62.

5. Kolata, *Clone: The Road to Dolly and the Path Ahead*, p. 34.

6. Lois Wingerson, *Unnatural Selection: The Promise and the Power of Human Gene Research* (New York: Bantam Books, 1998), pp. 48–49.

7. Ian Wilmut, Keith Campbell, and Colin Tudge, *The Second Creation: Dolly and the Age of Biological Control* (New York: Farrar, Straus and Giroux, 2000), pp. 210–211.

8. Margaret Lowrie, "19 European Nations Sign Ban on Human Cloning," *CNN Interactive*, January 12, 1998, <http://www.cnn.com/world/9801/12/cloning. ban> (July 1, 2002).

9. Leon R. Kass and James Q. Wilson, *The Ethics of Human Cloning* (Washington, D.C.: The AEI Press, 1998), p. xvi.

10. Kolata, *Clone: The Road to Dolly and the Path Ahead*, p. 228.

11. Ibid., p. 36.

12. Kass and Wilson, pp. xvi, xviii.

13. Nancy Gibbs, "Baby, It's You! and You, and You . . .," *Time*, February 19, 2001, p. 48.

14. "Forum on Human Cloning Turns Raucous," *Los Angeles Times*, March 10, 2001, p. 4A.

15. Wilmut, Campbell, and Tudge, p. 10.

Chapter 2. Cloning

1. National Bioethics Advisory Commission, "The Science and Application of Cloning," from Martha C. Nussbaum and Cass R. Sunstein, eds., *Clones and Clones: Facts and Fantasies About Human Cloning* (New York: W. W. Norton and Company, 1998), p. 21.

2. Lois Wingerson, *Unnatural Selection: The Promise and Power of Human Gene Research* (New York: Bantam Books, 1998), pp. 328–329.

3. Lee M. Silver, *Remaking Eden: Cloning and Beyond in a Brave New World* (New York: Avon Books, 1997), pp. 38–39.

4. Gina Kolata, *Clone: The Road to Dolly and the Path Ahead* (New York: William Morrow and Company, Inc., 1998), p. 25.

5. National Bioethics Advisory Commission, p. 30.

6. Ibid.

7. Ibid, p. 31.

8. Kolata, p. 146.

9. "How Scientists Created 'Dolly'," *CQ Research*, May 9, 1997, p. 413.

10. Ibid.

11. Ian Wilmut, Keith Campbell, and Colin Tudge, *The Second Creation: Dolly and the Age of Biological Control* (New York: Farrar, Straus and Giroux, 2000), p. 216.

12. "Timeline of Human Cloning," *University of Virginia Computer Science Department Page*, April 8, 1998, <http://www.cs.virginia.edu/~jones/tmp352/projects98/group1/timeline.html> (January 20, 2001).

13. Virginia Morell, "Cloning Offers New Hope for the Childless," from M. L. Rantala and Arthur J. Milgram, eds., *Cloning: For and Against* (Chicago and La Salle, Ill.: Open Court, 1999), p. 58.

14. "Embryo Cloning Approved in UK," *The Christian Century*, February 28, 2001, p. 13.

15. Silver, p. 105.

Chapter 3. Why Clone?

1. National Bioethics Advisory Commission, "The Science and Application of Cloning," from Martha C. Nussbaum and Cass R. Sunstein, eds., *Clones and Clones: Facts and Fantasies About Human Cloning* (New York: W. W. Norton and Company, 1998), p. 33.

2. Dan W. Brock, "Cloning Human Beings: An Assessment of the Ethical Issues Pro and Con," from Nussbaum and Sunstein, p. 146.

3. Ibid.

4. Ibid., pp. 147–148.

5. Nancy Gibbs, "Baby, It's You! and You, and You ...," *Time*, February 19, 2001, p. 48.

6. Gina Kolata, *Clone: The Road to Dolly and the Path Ahead* (New York: William Morrow and Company, Inc., 1998), p. 72.

7. Sharon Begley, "Cloning the Endangered," *Newsweek*, October 16, 2000, pp. 56–57.

8. Ibid.

9. Tom Harkin, "There Are No Appropriate Limits to Human Knowledge," from M. L. Rantala and Arthur J. Milgram, eds., *Cloning: For and Against* (Chicago and La Salle, Ill., Open Court, 1999), p. 118.

10. Ibid.

11. Ibid.

12. Kolata, p. 17.

13. Ibid., p. 18.

Chapter 4. Why Not to Clone

1. Gary Francione, "Animal Rights Commentary," *Animal Rights Law Project Page*, February 27, 1997, <http://www.animal-law.org/commentaries/fe2797.htm> (July 1, 2002).

2. National Bioethics Advisory Commission, "Religious Perspectives," from Martha C. Nussbaum and Cass R. Sunstein, eds., *Clones and Clones: Facts and Fantasies About Human Cloning* (New York: W. W. Norton and Company, 1998), pp. 168–169.

3. Eric A. Posner and Richard A. Posner, "The Demand for Human Cloning," from Nussbaum and Sunstein, pp. 235–236.

4. National Bioethics Advisory Commission, "Recommendations of the Commission," from Nussbaum and Sunstein, pp. 291–292.

5. R. C. Lewontin, "The Confusion Over Cloning," *The New York Review of Books*, October 23, 1997, pp. 18–24.

6. National Bioethics Advisory Commission, "Religious Perspectives," from Nussbaum and Sunstein, p. 170.

7. Ibid., p. 173.

8. Ibid., p. 171.

9. Leon R. Kass and James Q. Wilson, *The Ethics of Human Cloning* (Washington, D.C.: The AEI Press, 1998), pp. 25–27.

10. David Stipp, "Sex Is Still Necessary," from M. L. Rantala and Arthur J. Milgram, eds., *Cloning: For and Against* (Chicago and La Salle, Ill., Open Court, 1999), p. 188.

11. Ibid., pp. 188–189.

12. Lewontin, p. 20.

13. Lee M. Silver, *Remaking Eden: Cloning and Beyond in a Brave New World* (New York: Avon Books, 1997), pp. 103–105.

14. Thomas Wagner, "Dolly the Cloned Sheep Has Arthritis, Scientists Say," *The Associated Press*, January 4, 2002.

15. Nancy Gibbs, "Baby, It's You! and You, and You...," *Time*, February 19, 2001, pp. 56–57.

16. Kristen Philipkoski, "Cloning Ban Treaty Spurs Debate," *Wired News Page*, March 3, 2001, <http://www.wired.com/news/technology/0,1282,42108,00.html> (June 1, 2001).

17. Dan W. Brock, "Cloning Human Beings: An Assessment of the Ethical Issues Pro and Con," from Nussbaum and Sunstein, pp. 160–161.

18. Brian D. Johnson, "Self-Replication Is Big in Hollywood," from Rantala and Milgram, pp. 201–203.

19. Jonathan Beckwith, "Cloning Serves the Interest of Those in Power," from Rantala and Milgram, p. 225.

20. Ibid.

21. Gina Kolata, *Clone: The Road to Dolly and the Path Ahead* (New York: William Morrow and Company, Inc., 1998), p. 17.

22. The Christian Century, "Some Religious Leaders Would Permit Cloning of Humans," from Rantala and Milgram, p. 142.

23. Kolata, p. 159.

Chapter 5. Brave New World

1. Ian Wilmut, Keith Campbell, and Colin Tudge, *The Second Creation: Dolly and the Age of Biological Control* (New York: Farrar, Straus and Giroux, 2000), p. 266.

2. "Duplicate Dinner," *New Scientist*, May 17, 2001, <http://www.newscientist.com/dailynews/news.jsp?id=ns9999752> (July 1, 2002).

3. Sheryl Gay Stolberg, "Breakthrough in Pig Cloning Could Aid Organ Transplants," *The New York Times*, January 4, 2002, p. A1.

4. Nicholas Wade, "Genetic Code of Human Life is Cracked by Scientists," *The New York Times*, June 27, 2000, p. A1.

5. Kristen Philipkoski, "Cloning Ban Treaty Spurs Debate," *Wired News Page*, March 3, 2001, <http://www.wired.com/news/technology/0,1282,42108,00.html> (June 1, 2001).

6. Paul Recer, "Stem Cells Offer Distant Promise of Dazzling Medical Advances," Associated Press, August 10, 2001.

7. "Embryo Cloning Approved in UK," *The Christian Century*, February 28, 2001, p. 13.

8. Sheryl Gay Stolberg, "Total Ban on Cloning Research Appears Dead," *The New York Times*, June 14, 2002, p. A31.

9. "Europe Rejects Human Cloning Ban," *BBC News Page*, November 29, 2001, <http://news.bbc.co.uk/hi/english/sci/tech/newsid_1682000/1682591.stm> (July 1, 2002).

10. Jean Bethke Elshtain, "Cloning Humans Is Immoral," from M. L. Rantala and Arthur J. Milgram, eds., *Cloning: For and Against* (Chicago and La Salle, Ill.: Open Court, 1999), p. 150.

11. Nancy Gibbs, "Baby, It's You! and You, and You …," *Time*, February 19, 2001, p. 48.

chromosome—The structure within the nucleus of a cell that contains the genes necessary for the growth of an organism.

differentiated cell—A cell that has changed in form and has taken on the task that it has been assigned, such as creating skin, hair, muscle, or bone.

DNA (deoxyribonucleic acid)—The molecule of which genes are made.

enucleated cell—A cell that has had its nucleus removed.

gene—The unit that carries hereditary traits.

genome—The total arrangement of genes in an organism.

germ cell—A reproductive cell, either an egg or sperm cell, that does not change in form or function as the cell divides.

nucleus—The hard center of a cell that contains the chromosomes.

somatic cell—A body cell that changes in form and purpose as it divides.

undifferentiated cell—A cell that has not yet changed its shape or taken on any special task, such as creating skin, hair, muscle, or bone.

Glossary

Books

Cohen, Daniel. *Cloning*. Brookfield, Conn.: Millbrook Press, 1998.

Dudley, William. *The Ethics of Human Cloning*. San Diego: Greenhaven Press, 2001.

Edelson, Edward. *Francis Crick and James Watson: And the Building Blocks of Life*. New York: Oxford University Press, 1998.

Morgan, Sally. *Body Doubles: Cloning*. Chicago: Heinemann Library, 2002.

Nardo, Don. *Cloning*. Farmington Hills, Mich.: Gale Group, 2001.

Richardson, Hazel. *How to Clone a Sheep*. Danbury, Conn.: Franklin Watts, 2001.

Stanley, Debbie. *Genetic Engineering: The Cloning Debate*. New York: Rosen, 2000.

Internet Addresses

National Human Genome Research Institute
<http://www.ornl.gov/hgmis>

NewScientist Cloning Special Report
<http://www.newscientist.com/hottopics/cloning>

Roslin Institute
<http://www.roslin.ac.uk>

Further Reading

Index